Spiritual Exercises
A Short Primer on Mental Prayer

Jeffrey L. Morrow

Principium Institute   Toledo, Ohio

2017

Speaking with God: A Short Primer on Mental Prayer

Series: Principium Institute Resources for the Interior Life Volume 1

Copyright © 2017 Jeffrey L. Morrow. All rights reserved. No portion of this book may be reproduced without prior written permission from the author, with the exception of brief quotations with appropriate attribution provided.

Principium Institute
Toledo, OH

www.principiuminstitute.wordpress.com

ISBN: 9781520761978

Made in the U.S.A.

Speaking with God:
A Short Primer on Mental Prayer

Dedication

This booklet is dedicated to my mother, Cheryl Banks, who is the first person who taught me a prayer. That prayer began, *Baruch atah Adonai, Eloheinu melech ha-olam . . . Blessed art Thou O Lord, our God, King of the universe . . . .*

Contents

Acknowledgements	1
Introduction	3
1: What is Prayer?	7
2: How Do I Pray?	9
3: What Can I Pray About?	16
4: How Long Should I Spend in Prayer?	24
5: Where Should I Pray?	29
6: When Should I Pray?	32
7: Preparing for Prayer	36
8: Fighting Distraction	40
9: Beginning and Ending Well	45
Conclusion: The Importance of Prayer	50
Suggested Reading	54
Notes	57
About the Author	59

Acknowledgements

This booklet deals with the topic of mental prayer. I have learned about prayer, and more importantly, how to pray, from so many people over the years. The first person who taught me any prayers, was my mother, and thus, it is to her that I dedicate this short booklet. The first prayers I remember, were the Hebrew prayers that are traditionally said when lighting the candles on the menorah for Chanukah.

Eventually, I learned many more Hebrew prayers in preparation for my bar mitzvah. One of the most treasured prayers for me has been the *Shema*: *Shema Yisrael Adonai Eloheinu Adonai Echad . . . Hear O Israel, the Lord our God the Lord is One*—which I still pray every morning as part of my morning offering.

Biff Rocha and Jason Shanks were the first to teach me to pray in my own words, as a conversation with God. To them I owe more than I could ever repay. I continued to learn much about the ways of prayer from the writings of the Saints and masters of the interior life, especially: Pope St. John Paul II, St. Teresa of Avila, St. Francis De Sales, St.

John of the Cross, St. Ignatius Loyola, Thomas à Kempis, Brother Lawrence of the Resurrection, and St. Thérèse of Lisieux.

These were some of my most significant guides in my early years as a Christian in college and in graduate school. I also had many spiritual guides during these years, who helped provide me with the spiritual direction I needed, chief among them: Biff Rocha, the now Fr. Anthony Brausch, Fr. James Heft, S.M., and Fr. James Schimelpfenning, S.M.

In this little volume, however, most of the insights upon which I rely come from the spiritual guides I met later, especially John Coverdale, Fr. Robert Connor, Fr. Malcolm Kennedy, and Fr. Pablo Gadenz, as well as the writings of St. Josemaría Escrivá and of Blessed Alvaro del Portillo, both of whom John, Fr. Bob, and Fr. Malcolm knew personally. I draw quite freely from the ideas on prayer from these figures, especially from John, Fr. Bob, and St. Josemaría, so much so that it is safe to assume most of the material herein originates from one of them. I do not cite every instance of their inspiration and advice, because that would make this booklet cumbersome. I owe my wife Maria Morrow thanks for her editorial work revising this manuscript.

Introduction

What is prayer? What does prayer do? How does one pray? These are some of the basic questions this short booklet seeks to answer, as a short primer in prayer. The topics I will address include the basics of how to pray, about what to pray, where to pray, when to pray, and how to get the most out of prayer.

Different religious traditions view prayer differently, and they have different prayer "techniques." This booklet is written from the Christian perspective, and specifically from the Catholic tradition.
I will not be focusing so much on "techniques"

of prayer, as providing suggestions on how to get the most out of prayer given the concrete specifics of one's vocation and daily life, with all of its many demands.

Within the Catholic tradition, there are many forms of prayer: contemplative or vocal; spontaneous or memorized; *lectio* (prayerful reading) or simple quiet basking in the presence of God. In this volume, I focus on mental prayer, which is sometimes referred to as contemplative prayer. I am not speaking of mental prayer in the strict sense professional theologians of spirituality might, wherein time for mental prayer is strictly separated from vocal prayers. Rather, I am focusing on the practice of setting apart a fixed amount of time, ideally each day, to speak with God. In what follows, I sometimes include recommendations on involving vocal prayer or prayerful spiritual reading during the course of mental prayer.

After covering some of the basic introductory material about prayer, I discuss how to *do* mental prayer.
I then provide suggestions for how to pray well, in light of different states of life, different vocations, and different demands on one's time. These suggestions are best when adapted to one's own life circumstances. The

best context for making such decisions is that of spiritual direction. Of course, not everyone has the tremendous blessing of a spiritual director. In such circumstances, one might want to consider finding a priest or lay person who has admirable knowledge of the spiritual life. Such a person may provide wise counsel as to how best to incorporate prayer more effectively into one's regular routine.

This volume is intended to help the reader embark on a life of prayer. Ideally suited for the beginner new to the ways of prayer, I hope that even the saints among you might find something of benefit either for your own growth in the interior life, or for your guidance of other souls.

There is no one size fits all when it comes to the particularities of prayer. This is due in part to our differing life circumstances: living in a religious community where regular communal prayer punctuates the day; living near the Blessed Sacrament reserved in a tabernacle; being married; being single; having children; living childless; working a demanding job; seeking gainful employment; making a home and spending the bulk of the day caring for young children; never having prayed before; having a long-standing habit of spending hours a day in prayer; etc. We differ not only in vocation, occupation, and habits of prayer, but also in age, physical and mental abilities, health, and so many other ways.

Beyond these differences, however, God has created each of us out of love, and He has created us unique. No two of us are identical, and this is even true of identical twins who share genetic material and thus physical and other traits. Thus, God works with each of us differently, as do good parents with their individual children. Hopefully, no matter where you are on your journey with God, you will find something of benefit from these pages.

1: What is Prayer?

Prayer is simply relating with God. It can take the form of communicating directly (or indirectly) with God, or simply spending time with God. The American priest Fr. John Hugo, who was Dorothy Day's spiritual director, related a famous story about St. John Vianney, the patron saint of priests. St. John Vianney was the beloved nineteenth century parish priest in the small French village of Ars. A master of the interior life, and a confessor Saint who spent countless hours absolving sins in the confessional, St. John Vianney had an important encounter with a peasant in his parish. In Fr. Hugo's words:

> "The Curé of Ars, St. John Vianney, used to go to his parish church and he would always see there an old peasant man in rapt prayer. So one day he said to him,
> 'What do you do? How do you pray?'
> 'Well,' said the peasant, 'I look at him and he looks at me.'"[1]

Just basking in the presence of God can be a form of prayer. Throughout his pontificate, Pope Francis has spoken of the "gaze of Jesus," encouraging the faithful to simply allow the Lord to gaze on them from the tabernacle.[2]

In this booklet, we are focusing on mental prayer, which is a dialogue with the Lord. Such mental prayer is where we silently converse with our Lord. St. Teresa of Avila wrote of such prayer that:

> "Mental prayer in my opinion is nothing else than a close sharing between friends; it means taking time frequently to be alone with him who we know loves us."[3]

2: How Do I Pray?

"How do I pray?" I remember asking that question after I became an evangelical Protestant. I had been raised as a Jewish agnostic of sorts. Living in a Jewish home for some of my life, I knew a variety of prayers in Hebrew, although I often did not know what they meant. As an agnostic I was unsure whether or not any God existed that could hear my prayers. I was fairly certain, growing up, that such God probably did not exist.

I do remember one prayer, using my own words, from before my life as a Christian. I was very ill in a village in rural Honduras the summer after my junior year of high school when I was serving as a volunteer health worker building latrines. The gastrointestinal pain was so severe, I thought I was going to die. I later discovered I was suffering from both Giardia and E. coli. It was an unpleasant experience to say the least . . . I will spare you the details! At one point, during perhaps the worst moment, I spoke silently in my heart, "God, if you exist, please take this away."

My father, a physician, had provided me with some strong medication for just such an occasion, instructing me which symptoms would be appropriate for using the medicine. I had three of the four symptoms he mentioned. I attributed my healing solely to the medicine, and never gave that prayer—which I felt was uttered desperately under duress—a second thought until after I had come to faith in Jesus.

I said another prayer, using my own words, more than a year later. I had made the decision to do what evangelical Protestants often call, "accepting Christ," thanking Jesus for dying for my sins and asking Him to come into my life. This is often referred to as the "sinner's prayer."

It was after praying my makeshift "sinner's prayer" that I asked my Christian friends Biff and Jason, who had been co-leading the Bible study I was attending,

"How do I pray?" I explained to them my decision to follow Jesus, having committed my life to God with that "sinner's prayer," which I prayed at some point between 5 and 5:30 in the morning of Friday 5 of December 1997, after an all-night vigil of wrestling with the issue of Christianity, which had consumed my entire being that semester.

I had spent hours in thanksgiving, thanking God for the many wonderful things He provided both in the course of salvation history and in the course of my own life, as I was reflecting on my past in light of my newfound faith in God. I was a bit taken aback by Biff and Jason's response to my question. They replied, "Praying is just talking to God. You've been praying this whole time." It was that simple.

Perhaps my favorite line about prayer from the rich Christian spiritual tradition is from St. Josemaría Escrivá's first book composed of points for meditation, *The Way*, where he writes:

> "You don't know how to pray? Put yourself in the presence of God, and as soon as you have said, 'Lord, I don't know how to pray!' you can be sure you've already begun."[4]

Praying is that simple. It's just speaking with God. The Catholic tradition has a rich reservoir of memorized prayers that we can use for just about any occasion—prayers like the Our Father, the Hail Mary, the Glory Be, the Memorare. These vocal prayers are an important part of the Catholic spiritual tradition. But we can also use our own words, or even just lift our thoughts to God.

We can ask the Saints to pray for us, and this can be especially helpful at the beginning and end of our time of mental prayer; asking for the intercession of the Saints in heaven so that our time of prayer is fruitful, can help us pray well.

Mental prayer, however, is just about speaking with God; it is a dialogue between God our Father, and we His children. Again, I find St. Josemaría's comments helpful here:

> "You wrote to me: 'To pray is to talk with God. But about what?' About what? About him, and yourself: joys, sorrows, successes and failures, great ambitions, daily worries—even your weaknesses! And acts of thanksgiving and petitions—and love and reparation.
>
> "In short, to get to know him and to get to know yourself—'to get acquainted!'"[5]

I remember, not too long ago, my son Patrick was approaching his sixth birthday, and my son Robert was nearing his fourth birthday. I was putting them to bed, and it was time for us to pray. As I usually do each evening, I invited them to pray for anything they wanted to pray for, or for anyone.

Patrick responded, "Daddy, I don't know how to pray."

Before I could reply, Robert said, "Yes you do, silly. There's the Hail Mary, and the Angels of God prayer."

I asked Patrick, "What do you mean, you don't know how to pray? We pray every day."

Patrick clarified what he meant. "I mean, I don't know by heart any of the prayers we pray. And I don't really know what prayer is."

As a Catholic theologian, I was a little disheartened that my son didn't seem to know what prayer was. I felt slightly like a failure as a father! But I explained to both of them what I have been writing in these pages, namely that prayer is nothing other than speaking to God. Sometimes the words are not even necessary; prayer can be contemplating God, being aware of His presence, a smile. Prayer is relating to God. In mental prayer, we can be aided by our imagination, envisioning Jesus beside us as we speak with Him. Contemplating our Lord in this way while we speak can greatly aid our mental prayer.

Marriage and family life provide a host of analogies for our relationship with God. Spouses speak lovingly with one another. Sometimes they complain. Sometimes they ask for help. Sometimes they just listen. Other times they may simply embrace or sit next to one another in silence.

Even when I'm working away at my computer upstairs, knowing my wife Maria is downstairs provides a pleasant sense of presence in the background that is different from when she is out of the house. It can be similar with children relating to their parents. Children ask their parents for many things. Sometimes they say the sweetest things. Other times they complain and grumble. Children know when their parents are around.

It can be like this with God. When we spend time with God, aware of His presence, we are practicing a form of prayer, one often called, practicing the presence of God.[6] The important point for mental prayer, however, is that we put ourselves in the presence of God and don't hide anonymously in the crowd, rather relate to God directly, as

His beloved son or daughter whom He loved into existence. After all, that's what we are, a beloved child of God, the king and creator of the universe.

3: What Can I Pray About?

What's appropriate material for our prayer? What topics should we bring to prayer? We can bring just about any topic to our prayer. We should certainly have priorities in our prayer, but virtually any topic is fair game. What do I mean that our prayer should involve priorities? Well, first of all, since our prayer is about spending quality time with God, getting to know God better, we probably should not spend all of our time in prayer simply with prayers of petitions, that is, asking

God for things. Such prayers of petition are good, but our prayer life needs to consist of more than petitions. Furthermore, our priorities should be in the right place. For example, as a married man with six children at this point, I should probably spend more time praying about and for my wife and kids than about my career, my future, finances, etc. So, although we can and should pray about just anything, it would be beneficial for our prayer to concern the most important things *for me* to pray about *right now*.

Adoration

One important aspect of our time of prayer should be devoted to adoration. We should adore our Lord, speaking with Him affectionately from our heart, or telling Him loving words which we know we should pray, even if we feel spiritually dry at the moment. Such loving words and affectionate thoughts, are appropriate in our prayer with God, just as words of affection are appropriate in our married and family lives.

Atonement, Contrition, or Reparation

We need to tell God that we are sorry.

Our confession of sorrow for our present or past sins and faults should also play an important role in our relationship with God, and thus can be good material for our time of prayer. In our prayer we can also tell God we're sorry for the sins of others. These may not be sins others are guilty of—we don't know they're consciences, their will, their knowledge, and thus their culpability. But we read about and hear about objective offenses against God all the time. The evils of the world should not drive us to despair, but they should drive us to prayer. One thing we can do in our prayer, is tell God we're sorry when we encounter something objectively offensive, whether on our part or on someone else's behalf.

In the Book of Job we read that Job "would rise early in the morning and offer burnt offerings according to the number of them all [his children]; for Job said, 'It may be that my sons have sinned, and cursed God in their hearts.' Thus Job did continually" (1:5).[7]

We too, can tell God we are sorry, for ourselves and for others, offering Him various sacrifices as acts of reparation. Pope Francis remarked that:

> "The fragility of our era is this, too: we don't believe that there is a chance for redemption; for a hand to raise you up; for an embrace to save you, forgive you, pick you up, flood you with infinite, patient, indulgent love; to put you back on your feet. We need mercy."[8]

We need to know that God loves us, God will forgive us, and it is good for us to say we are sorry. This is something which is so important and yet our generation seems to be exceptionally bad at.

Thanksgiving

An important part of our prayer life should be thanking God for the many blessings we receive. One traditional Catholic prayer of thanksgiving after meals is, "We give Thee thanks, Almighty God, for these and all Thy benefits which we have received, Who lives and reigns, world without end, amen." It is good to thank God, just as it is good to thank others around us when they help us, do a kind act of service for us, etc. This post-meal prayer can be used at other times as well.

Supplication or Petition

It is also good to ask God for things. Our Lord Himself instructed us, "Ask, and it will be given you; seek, and you will find; knock, and it will be opened to you. For everyone who asks receives, and he who seeks finds, and to him who knocks it will be opened" (Matthew 7:7-8). It is good to ask God for things we think we need and want. Even better, however, is to ask God for what we really need. We may not know all the things we really need, but we know we are always spiritually in need; we always remain in need of God's graces.

Praying About Growth in the Spiritual Life

One important topic of our prayer should be the areas in which we need to grow spiritually. Perhaps we should pray about our dominant fault, either to discover what our dominant fault might be in order to root it out and develop the opposing virtue, or else to pray about ways of combatting that fault.

We should pray about the various spiritual commitments we may have made as part of our spiritual plan of life. Perhaps we need to make adjustments to our plan, adding something to it, or pruning it back. Maybe we do not need to make any additions or subtractions, but we simply need to pray better. For example, maybe we are going to Mass just the right amount, but we want to get more out of Mass. Or maybe we don't need to spend any more set minutes in prayer, but we want to get more out of our set times of prayer. Maybe we don't need to add another rosary, but we want to pray the rosary better. Our set time for mental prayer can be an excellent chance to spend some one-on-one time with the Lord and pray about how we can improve in the interior life.

    Another related area in this context pertains to our vocation. The celibate person can pray about concrete ways of living service to others. Those in religious community can pray about how better to serve the others with whom they live. A parish priest can pray about how best to serve his flock. The married person can pray about how he or she can express their love with concrete deeds to their spouse. The parent can pray about how best to help children to grow in a specific virtue. Regardless of one's state in life, the person needs to spend time in prayer asking the Lord for the light necessary to see how one can serve better the others around him or her: at home, at work, in the neighborhood, at the parish, etc.

In the context of spiritual direction, it is always a good idea to bring up how one prays, and the sort of things one prays about, but this is perhaps especially the case when trying to discover what God is asking of the person right now in order for one to move up the incline plane of the interior life, becoming increasingly a man or woman of prayer.

A Sharing Between Friends

Our prayer with God should be, as St. Teresa mentioned, "a sharing between friends." We can and should speak with God about what is important to us, just as our children speak to their parents about what is important to them. There are so many areas of our lives about which we can speak with God. We should speak about how best to help our family and friends, including especially how best to help them to grow closer to God.

We should be praying for the needs and intentions of the Pope, of our local bishop, of our pastor. We should be praying for our neighbors and colleagues at work. We should be praying for an increase in vocations to the priesthood and to religious life, as well as for holy marriages and for families to be schools of virtue, seedbeds of saints. Jesus told us, "The harvest is plentiful, but the laborers are few; pray therefore the Lord of the harvest to send out laborers into his harvest" (Matthew 9:37-38).

    We should also be praying about our temporal needs, and those of others, including the work we have to do, our financial and health concerns, etc. In short, God is our closest, most intimate friend, so we can speak with Him about all of the themes about which we would speak with our friends. We can share our joys, our sorrows, our anxieties, our hopes and dreams, as well as those of our family and friends.

4: How Long Should I Spend in Prayer?

The amount of time one should spend in mental prayer is going to vary greatly from person to person. The first point to keep in mind is that your time of mental prayer should not be your only form of prayer. The most important prayer for Catholics is the Mass. Members of religious orders and clergy pray the Divine Office, also known as the Liturgy of the Hours, or the Breviary, which is an important obligation for them. Those in contemplative religious communities will already be spending several hours each day in mental prayer.

For most Catholics, an hour a day is probably the upper end reasonable limit of time in mental prayer. For some, that hour might be taken all at once, whereas for others it might be divided into parts. One common way to spend an hour in mental prayer each day is to pray for half an hour at some point in the morning, and then for a second half hour at some point in the afternoon or early evening.

For those with busy work and family lives, a single session of half an hour, or two fifteen minute sessions of mental prayer, might even be a struggle, but a worthy goal. Not every Catholic will be able to devote an entire hour each day to mental prayer. Each individual will have to tailor their time of prayer to fit their other daily obligations.

In general, and it is best if this is brought to personal, individual spiritual direction so that it can be tailored for each individual's unique life circumstances, it is good to start small, and realistic, and move slowly up an incline plane over time. So there will not be a one *perfect* amount of time that each Catholic should spend in mental prayer each day. Every Catholic should spend some amount of time each day with God in prayer, but the amount of time, and when that will be, will differ from person to person.

Not everyone reading this book needs to spend more time each day in mental prayer. It is even possible that some might need to have less time set aside for prayer and more time for other duties: studies, work, family life, etc. Some individuals have a tendency to "over-spiritualize" their lives and neglect real duties of their state and vocation with prayer as an excuse. This is a danger. A good spiritual director will help guide an individual to cut back where they should cut back, and to put more effort into where they need more effort.

We may not all need to add more minutes of prayer each day, but we all can find room for improvement. None of us can say truthfully that we have arrived, we pray with the attention, spirit, and fervor of the greatest Saints. For some, my advice would be to do a little more than one's current practice . . . unless this is already an hour each day!

So, if one has never regularly spent a set amount of time in prayer with God before, he or she should probably start small. A good goal would be fifteen minutes each day. If that sounds like too much, then start smaller. Maybe try ten minutes, or even five minutes. I have yet to meet the person who cannot sacrifice five minutes a day to spend with God. Even single parents of large families can talk to God while rocking a child, or while driving in the car, etc.

Obviously, it is better to set aside silent time in an environment conducive to prayer, where one is doing nothing but speaking with God. But for the parent alone with children, who gets no break (not even to go to the bathroom alone), from the first moment their children woke them prior to their alarm, to the final moment where the parent woke up prematurely only to find that he or she fell asleep putting the kids to bed without finishing all of the household chores—the person has to make the best of what he or she has. God understands.

Over time, it would be good to work up to a half hour of time set aside for God in prayer. If one is single, or has a celibate vocation, an hour is a good goal. An hour is a good goal for the married and those with children as well, but it might be best to work slowly toward this goal over time. After all, there are other important aspects of the interior life besides mental prayer, like regular attendance at Mass, frequent confession, time for spiritual reading, the rosary, etc. For the religious and for the clergy, the Divine Office must take a very important place. Everyone, however, should make some time each day for mental prayer, to speak with the Lord and listen, basking in His presence. If we set aside some moments for God at fixed points throughout the day, we will better be able to live in God's presence the rest of the day.

5: Where Should I Pray?

One difficulty in beginning to spend time in prayer every day is the question of "where should I pray?" Again, as with virtually all of the advice in this booklet, there will not be one answer for each individual. In an ideal world, we would make the prayer in front of the Blessed Sacrament, the Eucharist. Nowhere else in this life can we be as close to our Lord than in proximity of His sacramental presence in our midst. If one lives in a religious community, or somewhere else where the Blessed Sacrament is reserved, then this should be relatively easy. If, like me, the person works at a Catholic institution where there is a chapel or oratory with a tabernacle—we have at least four on my campus, and probably more—then one might be able to spend some time in prayer during work hours, or just before work begins, or else before leaving for home.

What if one cannot get to a church, or the only time one is able to set aside for mental prayer is while at home or at work far away from the Blessed Sacrament? Fine. One can pray anywhere; it doesn't have to be in front of the Blessed Sacrament. God hears us wherever we are. Anyplace can be a sanctuary, and one does not need to set up holy pictures, or other human devices that aid prayer. One simply needs interior recollection. Ideally, the setting would be sufficiently silent to facilitate prayer. So, better your office, or your bedroom, than a coffee shop!

In the worst of circumstances, one really can pray anywhere, even amidst the hustle and bustle of the city streets while walking along, or while driving for long distances in the car. These are far from ideal circumstances, but if they are the best that a person has, it is better to spend a half hour of prayer in the car on the highway, than to leave the time of prayer until one is falling asleep, or until the next day. For many of us, especially if we have families, we may not spend all of our times of prayer in the same places.

The general rule, which we can all follow, is that we should pray in the best place that is realistically possible for us to pray: close to Jesus, silent, with as few distractions as possible. For some, that "best place that is realistically possible," at least on some days, might be while watching little kids play, with all the distractions that might naturally arise.

One should avoid making excuses, such as, "I can't make it to a chapel where the Blessed Sacrament is reserved," when perhaps the person can do this without that much effort. But at the same, time, one should not place unreasonable demands on oneself, especially if they negatively affect the others in one's life, like a spouse and children. This calls for prudence, and is another good topic for spiritual direction—"where should I spend my time in prayer on these days?"

6: When Should I Pray?

In general, it is good to have a fixed time for our prayer. Obviously, for many of us, this cannot be the same time each day. Perhaps the best time for me to pray one day, is when I am teaching class the next day. But if we do not set a time for our prayer and just wait until the ideal moment shows up, we are likely not to pray at all.

We want to find the best time to pray because we want to give God our very best. If one waits until going to bed for mental prayer, it is not likely to be very high quality of prayer, and it is possible that the person will even sleep through a significant portion of the time supposedly set aside for prayer! Praying right before bed is perhaps the worst time to pray as a daily commitment. If you are going to bed and you have not spent time in mental prayer yet that day, you might as well admit you missed your time of prayer for that day, but try for a better situation in the following day—one that allows for wakefulness and fulfilling the commitment. This is not to say that you can't pray while you're falling asleep.

I'm reminded of an anecdote I once heard about a man asking a priest if he can do another task while he prayed—intending his set time for mental prayer. The priest responded, "No, but you can pray during that other task." I could adapt that here just as easily. "Can I do my prayer while I'm lying in bed before falling asleep?" The answer would be, "No, but you can pray while you're lying in bed and falling asleep." It is good to give our last thoughts to God in the evening, but that is not the time for us to be doing our mental prayer for the day.

Everyone's schedule will be different. In general, it is probably a good idea to pray first thing in the morning. The reason for this is it helps the person give his or her first thoughts of the day to God. It helps one to start the day off on the right foot, and it ensures that nothing else gets in the way of this set time to pray with God. For those of us with young children at home, this often will be impossible. If one has a busy morning, with trying to get to Mass on time, trying to get to work on time, getting kids ready for school, etc., it might not be possible or advisable to spend the first half hour of your day in silent prayer. This is perhaps especially the case if you are already having to wake up early in the morning, like 6 a.m. or earlier.

When planning a schedule and trying to determine when would be the best time to do mental prayer, one should think about the time commitment to mental prayer as well as considering the location where one will be best able to pray. Perhaps it will be at church before Mass begins that day, or else at work just before seeing clients, or maybe during a lunch break or afternoon coffee break. It will vary person-to-person.

If one encounters unforeseen obstacles, like a sudden meeting not on the schedule, or something else, one should aim to rearrange the schedule as best as possible to allow time for prayer, and it is probably best to do the prayer as early as possible at that point.

Sometimes, these unforeseen changes in plans might require a person to be creative, and break up the time of prayer into smaller units. Maybe one can no longer do an entire half hour of uninterrupted prayer but could divide it into two sets of fifteen minutes, or three sets of ten minutes. When one can foresee the obstacles in advance, sometimes he or she will need to make sacrifices, like getting up earlier than normal, or skipping an activity that one enjoys and had planned on, but which is of less importance than prayer.

Of course, there will be times where we have to reduce our time of prayer, or omit it entirely, perhaps when we are ill, or when the demands of prudence and charity require it. Our time of prayer is intended to help our relationship with God and with others, to help us grow in the virtues, not become an obstacle to them.

7: Preparing for Prayer

It can be a good practice to prepare ourselves for our prayer. By preparation for prayer, I do not simply mean getting oneself into the proper state of mind—although that is important too, and we will discuss that more below when we come to beginning and ending our prayer well. What I mean here is scheduling our time, and also planning our topics for our prayer.

We need to schedule our time of prayer in advance. If we do not schedule when and where we will pray that day, then we are likely to skip our prayer. This is perhaps less of a problem for a contemplative living in a religious community. But it is a major challenge for those with busy family and work lives, and is also a challenge for parish priests. Many of the parish priests I know run very busy parishes, are often doing so alone without the assistance of other priests, and have numerous demands on their times.

The priests I know who spend time in mental prayer, in addition to their praying the Divine Office, sitting in a confessional, saying Mass, rosary, spiritual reading, etc., try to do so early, before the busy day begins. Some of them do a full hour early in the morning, others do an hour at a fixed point in the afternoon, somewhere where they will unlikely be disturbed, or they may do a half hour early in the morning, and a second half hour before dinner. The busier the work and family demands are, the more important scheduling times of prayer becomes.

It is not only important to prepare the time and place we plan on praying, but it can also be beneficial to prepare the topics of our prayer. Perhaps there are specific spiritual themes that we would like to contemplate: the fact that we are children of God, God is our loving Father; Jesus present in the Blessed Sacrament; our Lord's suffering and death for us; the mystery of the Trinity; the presence and action of the Holy Spirit in our soul; etc.

We might want to take to prayer some thoughts that emerged from our spiritual reading, or from our reading of Scripture, or the Mass readings for the day, from the day before or earlier that day. Maybe we had some resolutions from our last retreat, or some advice we received in the confessional or in spiritual direction. Maybe our family, friends, or colleagues have needs or prayer intentions for which we need to pray. Or perhaps we simply need light to see what God is asking of us at this moment: asking of us with regard to discerning a vocation or of living out our vocation. It is good to jot down some notes to take to our prayer so we don't have to rely simply on the strength (or weakness) of our memory.

We can also plan to bring to our prayer certain texts from Scripture or from a helpful spiritual text, for when we are overly tired or distracted in our prayer. Regardless of the specifics, preparing our time like this can help us so that we do not simply give in to distractions or waste time during our set time of prayer searching for a suitable topic about which to speak with God. Preparing in advance still allows us the freedom to deviate from our plan and discuss with God other more pressing matters that arose since we prepared our prayer, but it helps direct and focus our thoughts so we use our prayer time well.

8: Fighting Distraction

Distraction is one of the most challenging obstacles of those trying to develop a life of prayer. As the *Catechism of the Catholic Church* reminds us:

> "prayer is a battle . . . . Against ourselves and against the wiles of the tempter who does all he can to turn man away from prayer, away from union with God. We pray as we live, because we live as we pray."[9]

The first battle is to have the intention to pray. Without this desire, this intention, one will not pray. The next battle is to start to pray, to set aside the time and show up. The battle is not won, however, just by showing up, rather now the real battle begins. Distractions of all sorts enter in. Sometimes the distractions are in the form of sheer exhaustion. Other times the distractions may be flights of fancy, monologues or dialogues with the self rather than speaking with God, or even temptations to sin.

Notes on topics and themes, or of prayer intentions, which we bring to our prayer, can help us focus our thoughts. Another technique we can use is to rely upon a spiritual book that can help direct our attention to God. We can read certain passages and discuss them with God. This may not be ideal for mental prayer, but it is certainly better to speak with God about points from a spiritual text than to let one's mind wander aimlessly about.

That great master of the interior life, St. Teresa of Avila, had the following to say about this method:

> "My imagination is so sluggish that however hard I tried to think of or picture Our Lord's

human presence—and I tried very hard—I never succeeded.

"Now although, if they persevere, men may arrive more quickly at contemplation along this road where they cannot work with the intellect, it is a very laborious and painful one. For if the will is left without employment, and love has no present object to occupy it, the soul remains without support or activity, solitude and dryness give great pain, and stray thoughts attack most fiercely . . . . But anyone who cannot make use of this method runs a far greater risk, and should frequently resort to reading, since he can get help in no other way . . . .

" . . . . For I believe it would have been impossible for me to persevere for the eighteen years during which I suffered this trial and these great aridities, through not being able, as I have said, to meditate. All that time, except immediately after taking Communion, I never ventured to start praying with a book. My soul was as much afraid to engage in prayer without one, as if I had to fight against a host. With this protection, which was like a companion and a shield on which to take blows of my many thoughts, I found comfort, for I was not generally in aridity."[10]

My friend John Coverdale, who has provided me much guidance for my own soul and has done the same for many others over the decades, often phrases the right use of spiritual reading during times of mental prayer thus: "Read as little as possible, but as much as necessary." I think that is sage advice and right in line with St. Teresa of Avila's counsels.

Lots of texts could be used to help direct our thoughts during times of distraction in our mental prayer. The Scriptures, especially the Gospels, are probably the best. But virtually any good spiritual text, like the writings of the Saints, can be excellent choices. Some of the books mentioned at the end of this booklet could be good reading for distracted moments during mental prayer.

Another technique for dealing with distractions can be to use the invasive thoughts that pop into our mind as food for our prayer. Once we realize we are distracted, we can bring those distractions to our prayer, and then try to get back to where we were prior to becoming distracted. Or we could try meditating on a theme, or saying a vocal prayer, like the Our Father, very slowly, with serious attention. We can pause during portions of the prayer and contemplate what the words mean, speaking with God about each part of the prayer.

When none of these techniques works, we can repeat short vocal prayers of aspiration, little phrases. This is not, strictly speaking mental prayer, nor is spiritual reading, but it can become part of our mental prayer. Some of the Saints spent many hours of mental prayer over the years simply reciting such short vocal prayers because of distractions or spiritual dryness which sometimes occurred.

If our distractions are because we are tired, we need to take action fast. The first time our head begins to nod, or we find our eyes closing, we need to do something or we risk sleeping through our prayer. Perhaps we need to kneel for the duration of our prayer. Perhaps we need to stand up and finish our pray standing. Or maybe we need to walk around while we pray.

The point is to give it our best. When we get to heaven, we may discover that some of our best times of prayer were when we did not feel any consolations, when we were dry. In the end, our prayer is a response to God. God has a role to play in our times of prayer, and God does not lose battles.

9: Beginning and Ending Well

We should strive to begin and end our prayer well. If we begin our prayer well, with attention, we have a better chance of continuing to pray well for the rest of the time. Part of this is getting to prayer on time. Punctuality will help ensure that we actually spend our time in prayer, without cutting it short. In general, it is good to begin our prayer explicitly in the presence of God. In this context, our body position is important. It can be good to begin, and even end, kneeling, although this is not essential. It is especially appropriate to begin (and end) kneeling if we spend our time in prayer in front of the Blessed Sacrament.

In his justly famous *The Screwtape Letters*, C.S. Lewis wrote in the fictional person of a demon instructing another demon how to tempt Christians and lead them into sin:

> "At the very least, they can be persuaded that the bodily position makes no difference to their prayers; for they constantly forget, what you must always remember, that they are animals and that whatever their bodies do affects their souls."[11]

Our comportment and the way in which we hold ourselves, not only communicate to others, and in this case to the Other (God), the importance we attach to what we are doing, but in prayer, our posture does even more. As Scott Hahn writes:

> "Thus the soul expresses itself in our prayer,

whether private or liturgical, not only by our words but by our gestures and by the way we comport ourselves."[12]

Starting our prayer with good body posture—perhaps kneeling if we are able—is just one aspect of beginning our prayer well.

In terms of beginning in the presence of God, it can be quite helpful to start our prayer, our conversation with God, with a prayer that directs our thoughts to God's presence. I typically begin my times of mental prayer by making an act of the presence of God. Everyone is free to choose their own act of the presence of God prayer, or even to use their own words.

My prayer is this: "My Lord and my God, I firmly believe that you are here, that you see me, that you hear me." I try to say these words slowly and with affection. Often, I repeat them slowly several times at the beginning of my time of prayer, perhaps adding in other phrases, "that you love me, that you are concerned for me and for my family," etc. I follow that initial prayer with the following: "I adore you with profound reverence, I ask your pardon for my sins, and the grace to make this time of prayer fruitful." I then invoke our Lady, Saint Joseph, and my guardian angel to intercede on my behalf.

Ending our prayer well is also important. It is good to end on time. We need to be careful not to be a slave to our emotions. What I mean by that is we do not want to limit our prayer to the times we feel like praying, and thus cut our prayer short if we're just not into it, if we are just not feeling like praying right now. On the other hand, we should not prolong our prayer beyond the allotted time to which we committed in advance simply because we feel like praying. Most of us have duties beyond set times of prayer, and we need to get to work, or to get to class, or to spend time playing with our kids, etc.

Part of ending our prayer well can be that added emphasis on good posture, perhaps kneeling. Maybe we have discovered that, although we began our prayer with good posture, helping us be attentive to the Lord's presence, we have begun to slouch over during the prayer. As we approach the end of our time, it can be good to readjust our posture so that we can be extra attentive as we bring our set time of prayer to a close. I typically end with the following prayer: "I thank you my God for the good resolutions, affections, and inspirations that you have communicated to me during this meditation. I ask your help to put them into effect." Then, just as I had begun, I invoke the intercession of Mother Mary, St. Joseph, and my guardian angel.

Conclusion: The Importance of Prayer

In his *Last Testament*, Pope Emeritus Benedict XVI reflected on his own future death with the following words:

> "St. Augustine says something which is a great thought and a great comfort here. He interprets the passage from the Psalms 'seek his face always' as saying: this applies 'for ever'; to all eternity. God is so great that we never finish our searching. He is always new. With God there is perpetual, unending encounter, with new discoveries and new joy . . . . I think of these because it is very important to me to

believe that one is immersed in a great ocean of joy and love, so to speak."[13]

These words come not simply from Benedict XVI's deep theological learning, but ultimately, as he makes clear throughout his interview, they are the fruit of his daily prayer life.

A married saint from another era, St. Thomas More, had the following to say about the importance of spending some time in prayer each day:

> "If you are concerned for your well-being, if you wish to be safe from the snares of the devil, the storms of this world, the ambush of your enemies; if you long to be acceptable to God, if you crave to be happy at the last—then let no day pass without at least once making yourself present to God in prayer."[14]

Without prayer, we are lost. As a great saint from our own times, Pope St. John Paul II, put it:

> "*Prayer is a search for God*, but it is also *a revelation of God*. Through prayer God reveals Himself as Creator and Father, as Redeemer and Savior, as the Spirit who 'scrutinizes everything, even the depths of God' (1 Cor 2:10), and above all 'the secrets of human

> hearts' (cf. Ps 43[44]: 22). *Through prayer God reveals Himself above all as Mercy*—that is, Love that sustains, uplifts, and invites us to trust. The victory of good in the world is united organically with this truth. A person who prays professes such a truth and in a certain sense makes God, who is *merciful Love*, present in the world."[15]

Thus, for the Christian, prayer is not only an essential form of spiritual nourishment and sustenance, but an imperative obligation upon which so much hangs.

Such prayer, helps us to grow in love. The famous early twentieth century theologian of the spiritual life, Fr. Reginald Garrigou-Lagrange, O.P., who defined mental prayer as "the elevation of the soul to God,"[16] had the following to say about mental prayer:

> "It is through love that we seek to contemplate God, and the contemplation of the beauty and goodness of God increases our love. It is even necessary to say that here below contemplation is as a means to the end, in relation to love, since here below the love of God is more perfect than our knowledge of God."[17]

Writing further, Garrigou-Lagrange urges all to practice mental prayer:

"God calls all souls to the fountain of living water of mental prayer after a period of time . . . . I am speaking of that affective gaze of love that enables the soul to quench its thirst at the very fountain of life which is the Holy Spirit present in us."[18]

Those who embark on this life-long journey of mental prayer, are like ships setting sail on a marvelous adventure at sea, only the ocean of this voyage is nothing less than God Himself, the Author of life, Creator, and King of the universe.

Suggested Reading

Baur, Benedict. *In Silence with God*. Princeton: Scepter, 1997.

Boylan, Eugene. *Difficulties in Mental Prayer*. Princeton: Scepter, 1998.

Brother Lawrence of the Resurrection. *The Practice of the Presence of God*. Whitaker House, 1982.

De Sales, St. Francis. *Introduction to the Devout Life*. New York: Random House, 2002.

Escrivá, St. Josemaría. *The Forge*. New York: Scepter, 2011.

Escrivá, St. Josemaría. *Furrow*. New York: Scepter, 2011.

Escrivá, St. Josemaría. *The Way*. New York: Scepter, 2002.

Fernandez-Carvajal, Francis. *In Conversation with God: 7 Volume Set*. New York: Scepter, 1993.

Garrigou-Lagrange, Reginald. *Knowing the Love of God: Lessons from a Spiritual Master*. DeKalb: Lighthouse Catholic Media, 2015.

Giesler, Michael. *You See Me, You Hear Me: A Short Guide to Prayer for Young Adults*. New York: Scepter, 2013.

McDonough, Tom. *Learning to Pray with St. Josemaría*. Washington, D.C.: Clemency Press, 2014.

More, St. Thomas. *The Life of Pico Della Mirandola: "A Very Spectacle To All"*. New York: Scepter, 2011.

Philippe, Jacques. *In the School of the Holy Spirit*. New York: Scepter, 2007.

Philippe, Jacques. *Thirsting for Prayer*. New York: Scepter, 2014.

Philippe, Jacques. *Time for God*. New York: Scepter, 2008.

St. Teresa of Avila. *Interior Castle*. New York: Sheed and Ward, 1946.

Socias, James, ed. *Handbook of Prayers*. Chicago: Midwest Theological Forum, 2012.

NOTES

[1] David Scott and Mike Aquilina, ed., *Weapons of the Spirit: Living a Holy Life in Unholy Times: Selected Writings of Father John Hugo* (Huntington: Our Sunday Visitor, 1997), 92.

[2] Consider Pope Francis' discussion in his morning meditation in the chapel of the *Domus Sanctae Marthae* of Friday, 22 May 2015, entitled, "Three Manners of Gaze."

[3] St. Teresa of Jesus, *The Book of Her Life*, 8, 5 in *The Collected Works of St. Teresa of Avila Volume One*, 2nd rev. ed., trans. Kieran Kavanaugh, O.C.D. and Otilio Rodriguez, O.C.D. (Washington, D.C.: Institute of Carmelite Studies, 1987), 67. Here I have slightly modified the English translation.

[4] St. Josemaría Escrivá, *The Way*, no. 90, in St. Josemaría Escrivá, *The Way, Furrow, The Forge* (New York: Scepter, 2008), 21.

[5] Ibid., no. 91, in ibid.

[6] See, e.g., Brother Lawrence of the Resurrection, *The Practice of the Presence of God* (Whitaker House, 1982).

[7] All Bible translations taken from the RSVCE.

[8] Pope Francis, *The Name of God is Mercy: A Conversation with Andrea Tornielli* (New York: Random House, 2016), 16.

[9] *Catechism of the Catholic Church*, no. 2725, accessed on the Vatican website, http://www.vatican.va/archive/ccc_css/archive/catechism/p4s1c3a2.htm.

[10] St. Teresa of Avila, *The Life of St. Teresa of Avila by Herself* (New York: Penguin Books, 1957), 36-37.
[11] C.S. Lewis, *The Screwtape Letters* (New York: HarperCollins, 2000), 16.
[12] Scott Hahn, *Signs of Life: 40 Catholic Customs and Their Biblical Roots* (New York: Doubleday, 2009), 78.
[13] Pope Benedict XVI, *Last Testament: In His Own Words*, with Peter Seewald (London: Bloomsbury, 2016), unpaginated Kindle edition.
[14] St. Thomas More, *The Life of Pico Della Mirandola: "A Very Spectacle To All"* (Princeton: Scepter, 2010), 33.
[15] Pope John Paul II, *Crossing the Threshold of Hope* (New York: Alfred A. Knopf, 1994), 25-26.
[16] Reginald Garrigou-Lagrange, *Knowing the Love of God: Lessons from a Spiritual Master* (Lighthouse Catholic Media, 2015), 153.
[17] Garrigou-Lagrange, *Knowing the Love of God*, 156.
[18] Garrigou-Lagrange, *Knowing the Love of God*, 167-168.

About the Author:

Dr. Jeffrey L. Morrow is Associate Professor and Chair of the Department of Undergraduate Theology at Immaculate Conception Seminary School of Theology, at Seton Hall University in South Orange, New Jersey.

He is a Jewish convert to Catholicism. He first became an evangelical Protestant and then entered the Catholic Church at the Easter Vigil of 1999. He earned his B.A. in Comparative Religion and Classical Greek from Miami University, his M.A. and Ph.D. in Catholic Theology from the University of Dayton.

He serves as a Senior Fellow of the St. Paul Center for Biblical Theology, and is a Senior Fellow of the Principium Institute. He also is the main host of the History of Interpretation blog, and contributes frequently to the Caritas et Veritas blog. He is a popular speaker and has frequently presented at Franciscan University of Steubenville's summer conferences.

Made in the USA
Lexington, KY
13 March 2017